YOU CHOOSE BOOKS™

German Immigrants in America

An Interactive History Adventure

by Elizabeth Raum

Consultant:
Dr. Anke Ortlepp
Deputy Director, German Historical Institute
Washington, D.C.

Capstone
press®

Mankato, Minnesota

You Choose Books are published by Capstone Press,
151 Good Counsel Drive, P.O. Box 669, Mankato, Minnesota 56002.
www.capstonepress.com

Library of Congress Cataloging-in-Publication Data
Raum, Elizabeth.
    German immigrants in America : an interactive history adventure / by Elizabeth Raum.
    p. cm. — (You choose books)
    Summary: "Describes the experiences of German immigrants upon arriving in America. The reader's choices reveal historical details from the perspective of Germans who came to Texas in the 1840s, the Dakota Territory in the 1880s, and Wisconsin before the start of World War I" — Provided by publisher.
    Includes bibliographical references and index.
    ISBN-13: 978-1-4296-1356-9 (hardcover)   ISBN-13: 978-1-4296-1763-5 (softcover pbk.)
    ISBN-10: 1-4296-1356-4 (hardcover)   ISBN-10: 1-4296-1763-2 (softcover pbk.)
    1. German Americans — History — Juvenile literature. 2. Immigrants — United States — History — Juvenile literature. 3. United States — Emigration and immigration — History — Juvenile literature. 4. Germany — Emigration and immigration — History — Juvenile literature. 5. German Americans — Texas — History — 19th century — Juvenile literature. 6. German Americans — Dakota Territory — History — Juvenile literature. 7. German Americans — Wisconsin — Milwaukee — History — 20th century — Juvenile literature. I. Title. II. Series.
E184.G3R33 2008
973'.0431 — dc22   2007034225

Editorial Credits
Megan Schoeneberger, editor; Juliette Peters, set designer; Gene Bentdahl, book designer;
    Wanda Winch, photo researcher; Danielle Ceminsky, illustrator

Photo credits
The Bridgeman Art Library International/Giraudon/National Gallery of Art, Washington DC, USA, Lauros/Market Square, Germantown, Pennsylvania (oil on canvas), Britton, William (fl.1815-25), 102; Corbis, 91; Corbis/Bettmann, 95; Courtesy Gillespie County Historical Society, Fredericksburg, Texas, 23, 30; Courtesy of Kathleen Svoboda, www.volgagermans.net, 40; Courtesy of the Sophienburg Museum & Archives, New Braunfels, Texas, 10, 15, 24, 34; Courtesy Texas Parks & Wildlife, Interpretation & Exhibits Branch, 13; Daughters of the Republic of Texas Library, Yanaguana Society Collection, Block House, or Log Cabin, New Braunfels, Carl G. von Iwonski (1830-1912), SC96.009a, 19; Eureka Pioneer Museum of McPherson County, 61, 70; Getty Images Inc./Hulton Archive/FPG, 6; Getty Images Inc./Hulton Archive/MPI, 85; Library and Archives Canada/William James Topley, #PA-010254, cover; Library of Congress, 46, 72; Minnesota Historical Society/Loc# MB9.9 NU2 r6, 82; NDSU-NDIRS, Fargo, Fred Hultstrand History in Pictures Collection, 64; New York Public Library/Photography Collection, Miriam and Ira D. Wallach Division of Art, Prints and Photographs, Astor, Lenox and Tilden Foundations, 100; North Wind Picture Archives, 50, 56, 78; A painting of Norka, Russia by artist Michael Boss, www.volgagermans.net, 43; Wisconsin Historical Society/WHi-6908, 105; Wisconsin Historical Society/WHi-7439, 75

The author wishes to thank the following organizations for their help in preparing this book: Germans from Russian Heritage Society; North Dakota State Historical Society; Menno, South Dakota, Historical Society; NDSU: Germans from Russia Heritage Collection; German Heritage Foundation; Wisconsin Historical Society; Martin Luther College, New Ulm, Minnesota; the Gillespie County Historical Society; the Pioneer Memorial Library of Fredericksburg, Texas; and the interlibrary loan department of Harborfields Public Library, Greenlawn, New York.

1 2 3 4 5 6 13 12 11 10 09 08

TABLE OF CONTENTS

About Your Adventure..5

Chapter 1
Choosing America 7
Chapter 2
Taming Texas 11
Chapter 3
Homesteading...41
Chapter 4
A World at War...73
Chapter 5
German Americans 101

Time Line 106
Other Paths to Explore...108
Read More...109
Internet Sites..109
Glossary..110
Bibliography 111
Index 112

ABOUT YOUR ADVENTURE

YOU are a young German immigrant arriving in America. Opportunities as varied as the land itself await you. But struggles and hardships are waiting too. Will you succeed?

In this book, you'll explore how the choices people made meant the difference between life and death. The events you'll experience happened to real people.

Chapter One sets the scene. Then you choose which path to read. Follow the directions at the bottom of each page. The choices you make will change your outcome. After you finish one path, go back and read the others for new perspectives and more adventures.

YOU CHOOSE the path
you take through history.

In the early 1900s, immigrants crowded onto ships sailing to America.

Choosing America

"There!" someone shouts. "America!"

You peer across the water and see the hazy outline of land on the horizon. "When will we arrive?" you ask.

"Tomorrow," a woman answers.

It's been a difficult journey. You had barely left the German port of Bremen before the ship hit rough seas. You fought to keep your balance as giant waves tossed you from side to side. Many passengers became seasick. "I never should have left German soil," one man moaned.

Turn the page.

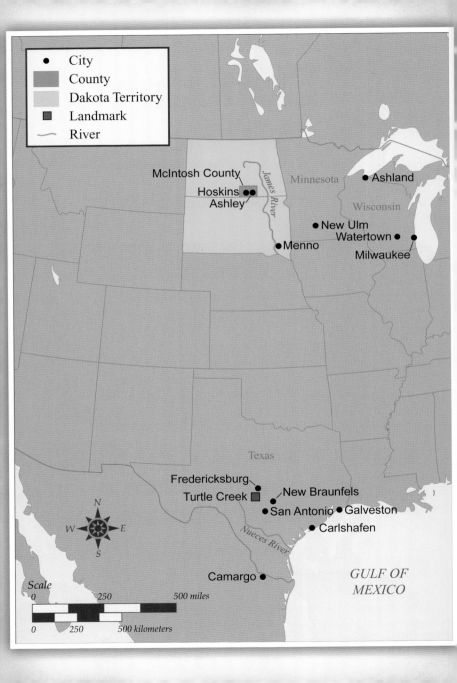

For years, you have dreamed of coming to America. You've read books and heard stories of a life filled with adventure and opportunity.

But now that you can see America in the distance, you wonder if you made the right decision. What will life be like in America? You speak German. Will Americans understand you? Will you understand them?

No one has promised that life in America will be easy. You expect to face hardships of one kind or another. All immigrants do. Do you have the courage you'll need to overcome hardships and make a new life for yourself?

➤ To learn what life was like for Germans in Texas in the 1840s, turn to page **11**.

➤ To join Germans from Russia homesteading in Dakota Territory in the 1880s, turn to page **41**.

➤ To experience being a German immigrant during World War I (1914–1918), turn to page **73**.

Carlshafen became the city of
Indianola, Texas, in 1846.

CHAPTER 2

Taming Texas

Your ship, the *Herschel*, docks at Galveston, Texas, on October 22, 1845. The captain points out a smaller boat. "That will take you to Carlshafen, the Adelsverein camp on Indian Point," he says.

The Adelsverein, or the Society for the Protection of German Immigrants, is a group of German noblemen. They charged only $120 for passage to Texas. The society then promised you 320 acres of land, a house, and enough supplies to last you a year. They are calling their new settlement "the new Fatherland on the other side of the ocean."

Turn the page.

Popular German novels like Charles Sealsfield's *The Cabin Book* describe Texas as a place of hope. It is the place where settlers overcame the much larger Mexican army in 1836. The settlers created the independent Republic of Texas. Now, Texas is about to become a state. It is a place where you can be in charge of your own fate.

You carry two heavy boxes of woodworking tools off the *Herschel*. Other passengers wrestle pianos, grandfather clocks, and heavy furniture off the ship and onto a smaller boat.

Once everything is cleared off the *Herschel*, you shake the captain's hand. "Good luck!" he says.

"You'll need all the luck you can get," a sailor sneers. "Are your leaders, the Adelsverein, ready to fight the Comanche?"

Comanche Indians had lived in Texas since the 1700s.

You've heard about the Comanche. They are the most powerful American Indian tribe in Texas. Settlers have tried for years to make treaties with them. But the settlers won't give in to the Comanche's single demand — a boundary line between Texas and the Comanche's traditional hunting land. As a result, Comanche warriors have attacked several settlements.

Turn the page.

You're about to board the boat to Carlshafen when a man approaches you. "Do you have tools there?" he asks in German.

"I made furniture in Germany," you say.

"Wonderful! My name is Johann Ahrens, and I am looking for a furniture maker for my shop here in Galveston. I'd love to hire a fellow German. Would you like a job?"

Talk about being in the right place at the right time! If you take the job, you won't have to worry about Comanche attacks. On the other hand, the Adelsverein promised to protect you. You have no reason not to trust the Adelsverein's promises.

➤ *To keep going to Carlshafen, go to page 15.*

➤ *To stay in Galveston, turn to page 35.*

Prince Carl of Solms-Braunfels was a German nobleman who started the Adelsverein.

You thank Ahrens for his offer, but you board the boat. You need to give the Adelsverein a chance.

It is a 100-mile trip down the coast to Carlshafen. Last year, Prince Carl of Solms-Braunfels, the Adelsverein leader, welcomed a small group of Germans to Carlshafen. From there, they traveled inland and started the town of New Braunfels.

Turn the page.

At Carlshafen, you unload the boat. "We'll wait here until the weather is better for travel," one man says. "Then wagons will be along to take you to New Braunfels."

But after two months, you are still stuck at Carlshafen. Christmas comes and goes. While you wait, more immigrants arrive from Germany. By January 1846, there are 4,000 German settlers waiting at Carlshafen. In all this time, there has been no sign of the wagons.

"What kind of a leader is Prince Carl, to leave us stranded here for so long?" you ask.

"Prince Carl has gone back to Germany. There's a new leader now," one man says.

"Who is it?" you ask.

"His full name is Baron Otfried Hans Freiherr von Meusebach. But he goes by the name of John Meusebach."

"I don't care who the leader is. I've had enough," says another man. "I'm going back to Galveston."

Returning to Galveston isn't a bad idea. If you're lucky, maybe Ahrens will still hire you.

But what if Meusebach is more organized? The wagons could come any day now. You've got land waiting for you when they do.

⇢ *To wait a little longer, turn to page* **18**.

⇢ *To take the next ship back to Galveston, turn to page* **34**.

You decide to wait. Finally, Meusebach sends wagons in March 1846. But there's a problem. There are only enough wagons for 1,000 people. "What about the other 3,000?" you ask.

"More will come later," a driver says.

You're lucky to find a place in one of the wagons. But before you leave, a young man asks for your seat. "My father and brother are already on the wagon," he says. "The three of us want to stay together." He offers you money.

It's a generous offer, enough for you to set up your own shop. But the next wagons could take weeks, even months.

➤ *To keep your seat, go to page* **19**.

➤ *To give up your seat, turn to page* **21**.

Many early settlers in New Braunfels were farmers.

"I won't sell my seat," you tell the young man.

It takes two weeks to reach New Braunfels. It feels good to eat German food, sleep in a warm log cabin, and rest.

Meanwhile, Meusebach has been planning a second settlement 60 miles northwest of New Braunfels. He names the new town Fredericksburg after a member of the Adelsverein.

Turn the page.

On May 8, 1846, you are among the first group of 120 settlers to arrive in Fredericksburg. Each settler receives one lot in town and 10 acres of farmland nearby. By the end of the summer, hundreds more people have reached Fredericksburg.

So far, trade with the Comanche has been peaceful. But as more Germans arrive, the future of the settlements depends on a treaty. Meusebach plans to meet with the Indian leaders in March. You could go with him, but it might be dangerous. You've heard the Comanche are preparing for war. Will you join him?

➤ To stay in Fredericksburg where you feel safer, turn to page 23.

➤ To join Meusebach as he tries to arrange peace with the Comanche, turn to page 24.

"I'll take the next wagon," you say as you sell your seat.

But the next wagon never comes. In May, the United States declares war on Mexico. The dispute is over the exact location of the southwestern border between Texas and Mexico. The United States claims that the border follows the Rio Grande river. Mexico thinks it is farther north. For the war, the army needs wagons. There are no wagons left for the Adelsverein to send.

One of the men, Augustus Buchel, decides to form a company of soldiers to fight the Mexicans. "We can join the army. At least soldiers get good food and uniforms," he says.

"I didn't come to Texas to be a soldier," you say.

Turn the page.

"It's better than dying here," Buchel says.

"The Adelsverein still owes us land. Why don't we walk to New Braunfels and claim it?" someone suggests.

It's 150 miles to New Braunfels. But at least you wouldn't have to join the army. Which will you choose?

→ To join the army, turn to page 26.

→ To walk to New Braunfels, turn to page 28.

The Vereins-Kirche in Fredericksburg was a traditional German building with eight sides.

You decide to stay in Fredericksburg while the others go to the Comanche village. While you wait for news, you help build the Vereins-Kirche on Main Street. This eight-sided wooden building will be used for church, school, and community meetings.

Meanwhile, Meusebach's plan to make peace with the Comanche leaders works. The threat of Comanche attacks is gone.

Turn to page 30.

On January 22, 1847, you and a small group of settlers leave Fredericksburg with Meusebach. You reach the Comanche village in February. Buffalo-skin tepees dot the village. A large herd of horses grazes nearby.

John Meusebach arranged a treaty with Comanche leaders.

On March 1, 1847, Meusebach meets with Comanche leaders Buffalo Hump, Santa Anna, and Old Owl. Through Jim Shaw, an Indian guide who speaks the Comanche language, Meusebach offers $3,000 worth of presents. In exchange, the Comanche agree to leave the Germans alone. With the treaty, Meusebach finally succeeds where so many others had failed.

You return to Fredericksburg. With the threat of Comanche attacks gone, you decide to build a house.

Turn to page **30**.

On May 22, 1846, you join the First Texas Rifle Volunteers under Captain Buchel. You become friends with Emil Kriewitz, a fellow soldier. Kriewitz, like you, came to Texas with the Adelsverein.

In late July 1846, you reach Camargo, Mexico, where General Zachary Taylor is camped with the United States forces.

Your unit is especially hard hit with an outbreak of yellow fever. "We're losing more men to fever than to battle wounds," the commanders say. Doctors can't say for sure what causes the sickness. Many people think the bad air of the swamps has something to do with it. To you, the cause doesn't matter. What matters is that most of the men in your unit have died from the sickness.

By fall, the commanders send what's left of your unit home. But where is home? Germany or Texas?

Back at Carlshafen, you learn that Meusebach is planning to meet with Comanche leaders to make a peace treaty. The Adelsverein hires your friend Emil Kriewitz to guard Meusebach. "The Texans say a treaty will never happen," Kriewitz tells you, "but Meusebach is determined to try. Do you want to come along?"

It sounds exciting, but you also think about returning to Galveston. Maybe you could still get a job as a furniture maker.

➻ To help guard Meusebach, turn to page 33.

➻ To catch the next boat back to Galveston, turn to page 34.

You begin the long walk inland without food, warm blankets, or water. Many of your fellow travelers are sick.

You are angry with the Adelsverein. "Why aren't they helping us?" you ask.

"They claim to be out of money," one of your fellow travelers answers.

By the time you reach New Braunfels, more than 1,000 of your fellow travelers have died. And now you don't feel well, either. Your joints hurt, you can't eat, and your gums are bloody. You go to the town's doctor.

"You have scurvy," Dr. Koester says. The doctor tells you to rest and eat what you can.

A friend offers you a bed and urges you to eat. Despite his kindness, your sickness worsens. You ache all over.

"Will you write to my parents?" you ask. "Tell them what happened to me."

He nods. A few hours later, you die of scurvy.

THE END

To follow another path, turn to page 9.
To read the conclusion, turn to page 101.

Fredericksburg was the Adelsverein's second settlement in Texas.

Soon, you open a furniture shop on Fredericksburg's Main Street. Bakeries, a general store, a blacksmith shop, and the hotel are nearby.

During the 1850s, the issues of slavery and states' rights split the country. People in the North want to end the practice of slavery in the United States. But Southerners depend on slavery to get work done cheaply. If costs go up, goods will be more expensive. They argue that each state should have the right to decide whether or not to allow slavery.

In February 1861, Southern states, including Texas, break ties with the United States. They form their own nation, the Confederate States of America. America is divided between the Union of Northern states and the Confederacy of Southern states. By April, the two sides are fighting the Civil War.

Turn the page.

By law, all men between the ages of 17 and 50 must serve in the Confederate Army. There are rumors of soldiers kidnapping young German men and burning their homes as punishment for not joining the Confederacy.

You do not want to fight for the South. Several businessmen in Fredericksburg make plans to escape to Mexico until the war ends. Anyone wishing to make a run for Mexico is to meet August 1, 1862, at Turtle Creek. Is it worth the risk?

➤ *To go to Turtle Creek, turn to page* **36**.

➤ *To stay in Fredericksburg, turn to page* **37**.

You leave with Kriewitz in January 1847. Meusebach has already left for the Comanche village. "March!" Kriewitz commands, but you can't catch up to Meusebach.

You finally meet up with Meusebach as he returns to Fredericksburg. He tells you that his meeting with the Comanche leaders was a success. They agreed to leave the Germans alone in exchange for $3,000 in goods.

In Fredericksburg, Meusebach offers you land in the town and 10 acres just outside town.

But by this time, several men have already opened furniture shops. A friend encourages you to move to San Antonio. "It's a growing town. There will be new opportunities there."

➤ To stay in Fredericksburg, turn to page **38**.

➤ To move to San Antonio, turn to page **39**.

Many Germans opened furniture stores in America.

You return to Galveston. At the busy port, slaves unload cotton from mule-drawn wagons and carry it onto ships. You pass warehouses, banks, hotels, and trading companies. Several shops sell furniture, but you finally find Ahrens' shop.

"The job's still available," Mr. Ahrens says.

What luck! You're not going to miss this second chance. "I'll take it," you say.

At Ahrens' shop, you build pine tables, beds, desks, and cupboards. You use traditional hand tools and foot-powered turning lathes. Building furniture by hand allows you to pay close attention to the smallest details.

Over time, factories with steam-powered machinery begin to take the place of hand tools. The factories produce large amounts of furniture at low prices. To compete, Ahrens hires more workers and buys a horse-powered lathe. You miss making furniture by hand.

You marry and have a family. All the furniture in your house is made by hand, the old-fashioned way. "Progress is fine for others," you say, "but I like the old German ways best."

THE END

To follow another path, turn to page 9.
To read the conclusion, turn to page 101.

You join about 65 men who gather at Turtle Creek. You elect Fritz Teneger to lead the group, and the group heads southwest. Certain you are not being followed, you travel at a slow pace. On August 9, 1863, you stop to camp along the banks of the Nueces River.

Early in the morning, shots wake you. "Confederate soldiers!" someone yells. In the darkness, you make out the shadows of almost 100 Confederate soldiers.

At first light, the soldiers charge. You try to hold your ground, but the soldiers are too quick. Some of your fellow Germans escape into the woods. You start to follow. As you run, you are hit with a bullet. You die in what will come to be known as the battle of the Nueces.

THE END

To follow another path, turn to page 9.
To read the conclusion, turn to page 101.

You decide you'll be safer in Fredericksburg. After just two days, the Confederates learn of the escape plan. Lieutenant C. D. McRae and about 100 soldiers catch up to the Germans on August 9 at the Nueces River. In a battle the following morning, at least 19 Germans die. Nine more are killed a few hours later.

You're glad you stayed in Fredericksburg to run your business. As an extra precaution, you take an oath of loyalty to the Confederacy. You are careful not to say anything about slavery.

You rejoice when the war ends in April 1865. Now you can focus on your business, free to say and do whatever you want.

THE END

To follow another path, turn to page 9.
To read the conclusion, turn to page 101.

You decide to stay. In the spring, you plant corn and cotton. Your crops do well, so you buy more land.

Meusebach's treaty with the Comanche ends as new settlements continue to creep into the Comanche's hunting grounds. Attempting to save their land, the Comanche attack settlers. In 1848, the U.S. Army builds Fort Martin Scott near Fredericksburg. You feel safer with soldiers nearby.

By 1850, the buffalo are disappearing, and so is the Comanche way of life. In a few years, the government will move the Comanche to reservations. The days when Germans and Comanche lived side by side in peace are gone forever.

THE END

To follow another path, turn to page 9.
To read the conclusion, turn to page 101.

Many of the new settlers in San Antonio are German. You open a furniture shop of your own. You also begin making wagons. You soon have more orders than you can fill. You become one of San Antonio's leading businessmen.

In the years to come, many of the city's wealthy Germans build houses along King William Street. You are among them. The fashionable neighborhood soon becomes the heart of the German community in San Antonio.

You've done well in Texas. Although you'll never forget your German roots, you are a Texan now.

THE END

To follow another path, turn to page 9.
To read the conclusion, turn to page 101.

Families kept their German traditions after moving to Russia.

CHAPTER 3

Homesteading

You reach New York's Castle Garden Immigration Center in May 1887. A train takes you from New York to Dakota Territory. Between the small towns, a flat, treeless prairie stretches as far as you can see. The grasses are taller, but otherwise it looks much like the Russian steppe you left behind.

The train is crowded. At night, you and your brothers sleep in the aisles of the train with Papa. Mama and the little ones sleep in the seats.

The conductor steps over you. "Russians," he sneers.

"Not Russian," Papa says proudly. "German."

Turn the page.

You smile. Although you lived in Russia, you are proud to be German. Your great-grandparents and many other Germans settled near Russia's Black Sea more than 100 years ago. They clung tightly to their German identities. You speak German, not Russian.

The Germans had moved to Russia at the invitation of the Russian leader Catherine the Great. She promised free land, freedom of religion, and freedom from the military. But the newest leader, Alexander II, broke all of Catherine's promises. Papa decided to leave Russia the day he heard his sons would have to serve in the Russian army.

Word of free land in America reached your village. Your uncle was the first of your family to leave. He wrote letters describing the open, unsettled prairie in Dakota Territory. "Wheat grows well here. Bring seeds," he wrote.

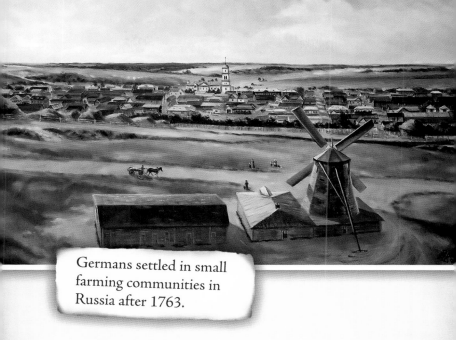

Germans settled in small farming communities in Russia after 1763.

Your parents sold the family farm. Mama sewed the money from the sale into the hems of her skirt and Papa's coat. Then you traveled to Bremen, Germany. From there, you sailed to New York.

Turn the page.

After a four-day train trip, you reach the town of Menno in Dakota Territory. Your uncle meets you at the station and brings you to his sod house a few miles away. Your aunt serves fried sauerkraut, potatoes, and pork. The German food and conversation almost makes you forget you are in a strange new place.

Papa asks your uncle about getting land. "Is it truly free?"

"Almost," your uncle answers. "You must pay a fee of about $10." He tells you about a law called the Homestead Act. Any person 21 or older who is the head of a family can file a claim on 160 acres of unsettled land. You must improve the land by building a home and growing crops. After five years, the land will be yours. "Much of this free land is up north in McIntosh County. In fact, many families have left Menno to claim it."

"And what of the land around Menno?" Papa asks.

"Most of the homestead land has been taken. But there are abandoned farms for sale."

Mama says, "It would be nice to stay near family."

Papa says, "But the free land sounds like a dream come true. I'm not sure which to choose." He turns to you and your brothers. "What do you think?"

➺ To suggest staying in Menno, turn to page **46**.

➺ To encourage Papa to go north, turn to page **49**.

Settlers built dugout houses into hillsides.

"The farmland here is already plowed," you point out. "We could plant our seeds sooner."

"You make a good point," Papa says. His praise fills you with pride. "We will stay," he finally decides.

He buys an abandoned farm near the James River. It has a tiny dugout house and a small barn. Logs brace the walls and form the roof and doorway.

You help plant a small field of wheat with the seeds you brought from Russia. Papa works for the blacksmith in town. While Papa works, everyone else must run the farm.

As summer fades to fall, you and your brothers harvest the wheat. After the harvest, you prepare for winter. Firewood is hard to find on the treeless prairie. Instead, you gather prairie grass. When twisted, it burns slowly and well.

With fewer daily chores to do, you finally have time for school. Your neighbors hire a teacher. Their small sod hut serves as the school building. Nine students sit at a long table. They range in age from 6 to 20.

Turn the page.

January 12, 1888, starts out unusually warm. But shortly after lunch, the temperature drops suddenly. Wind blasts across the prairie, and snow begins falling. The teacher dismisses school early. She wants you to walk home before the storm gets any worse.

But you had questions about the day's lesson. You were hoping to get some help from the teacher after class. You look outside. The snowfall is heavy, but not too bad. You can still see your family's barn in the distance. You can probably delay a few minutes and still make it home safely.

→ To try to get home right away, turn to page **54**.

→ To stay and get help from the teacher, turn to page **55**.

"I think we should take advantage of the government's offer," you say. You are filled with pride when Papa agrees with you.

Papa buys oxen, a wagon, a plow, and a few tools. You load everything in the wagon and say goodbye to your aunt and uncle. The oxen plod along slowly at about 2 miles an hour. The trip to McIntosh County takes two weeks.

Papa claims land about 4 miles west of the city of Hoskins. "This will be the perfect place to plant the hard red wheat seeds we brought from Russia," Papa says.

Once the seeds are planted, you help Papa build a sod hut. You cut huge slabs of prairie soil and pile them up to form the walls. Papa braces the roof with lumber. Then you and your brothers lay more sod on top. The hut takes three days to build.

Turn the page.

Fires were a constant danger on the dry prairie.

The summer is hotter than expected. Weeks pass without any rain. Clouds form occasionally over the thirsty prairie, but they disappear without giving up so much as a drop.

One night, you notice a red glare in the sky.

"Fire!" your brother shouts. "Prairie fire!" The fire is heading straight for your farm, and it's burning fast.

"We fight fire with fire," your father shouts. "Light small fires in the path of the big fire. When they meet, they will burn each other out."

That doesn't make sense to you. What if something goes wrong? Maybe you should wait to see if the fire will turn away.

→ *To light the fires, turn to page* **52**.

→ *To wait for the fire to turn, turn to page* **53**.

You can't just stand by. You and your brothers rush to light the small fires. The prairie fire roars closer and closer. Suddenly, it meets the backfires. WHOOSH! Sparks fly high into the sky. The fire burns out, leaving darkness and smoke. Your home, wheat field, and animals are saved.

In August, you harvest the wheat. Papa sells it in town, but prices are low. He doesn't get as much money as he had hoped. By September, cold prairie winds signal the upcoming winter.

Papa isn't sure the family will have enough money to buy supplies to make it through to spring. He decides to go to Hoskins to borrow money. You go with him.

Turn to page 58.

"How do we know our own fires won't destroy our fields?" you ask. You convince Papa to wait a little longer.

The fire roars closer and closer. After a few minutes, the rushing fire seems to turn. You sigh with relief. But at the last minute, the fire turns again. You don't have time to light backfires. You barely have enough time to get out of its way.

There's nothing you can do. The wheat is gone. It's too late in the growing season to start over.

"Without the wheat to sell, how will we buy supplies for winter?" Mama wonders.

"We have no choice but to borrow money," Papa says. The next day, you and Papa walk to Hoskins.

Turn to page 58.

You are about halfway home when the wind shifts. Heavy snow swirls around you. Your family's barn disappears in a blanket of white.

Your cheeks tingle. So do your fingers and toes. You struggle forward through deepening banks of snow. Exhausted, you stop to rest. You watch the snowflakes as they seem to dance to the music of the howling wind. Slowly, you fall asleep.

Your family doesn't find you until the next morning — frozen to death and lying in the snow 10 feet from the dugout's door.

You are not the only one to die in the blizzard. Many settlers freeze to death in the prairie storm.

THE END

To follow another path, turn to page 9.
To read the conclusion, turn to page 101.

You ask your teacher to explain the lesson one more time. Just as she finishes, the sun disappears behind thick black clouds. The room darkens. You look outside, but you can't see a thing through the blanket of swirling snow.

"You two better wait here until the storm ends," your neighbor says to you and your teacher. Everyone huddles by the family's stove as snow piles up outside.

After a few hours, the storm shows no sign of weakening. "The cow will need milking soon," your neighbor says. He puts on his heavy coat and prepares to go outside.

"But how will you find the animal shed through the blowing snow?" you ask. "What if you get lost?"

In winter, heavy snows covered
the treeless prairie.

Your neighbor ties a piece of heavy rope
to the door frame. Then he ties the other end
around his waist. "If I lose my way, I'll just
follow this rope back to the hut. Once I reach
the shed, I'll tie it to the cow's stall. When I
finish the chores, I'll follow the rope home."
The plan works. Your neighbor returns safely
after completing his chores.

The wind howls through the night. By
morning, the storm is finally over.

That afternoon, the door bursts open. A blast of freezing air fills the room. It's Papa! "I brought the wagon to bring you home," he says.

The spring of 1888 is cool. Rivers and streams swell with the melting snow. Wildflowers bloom on the roof of your house.

One morning, your uncle visits. "We have decided to move north. I'm told that the land there is even better for growing wheat. Would you like to join us?"

"We have done well in Menno," Mama says. "Let's stay here."

Papa doesn't ask your opinion, but you decide to speak up.

➸ To convince Papa to stay in Menno, turn to page **60**.

➸ To convince Papa to go north, turn to page **63**.

In Hoskins, Papa heads to the McIntosh County Bank to borrow money. You wander down Main Street. Two men in front of Mr. Gulack's general store speak to each other in English. You can't understand them. Suddenly, you bump into someone.

"*Entschuldigung*," you say, forgetting that few people here can understand your German way of saying "excuse me."

"Are you new to town?" the woman asks in German. When she sees the surprised look on your face, she adds, "My grandparents came from Germany many years ago."

"We came in June." You tell her all about your family, the fire, and Papa's worries about having enough money.

"I'm so sorry," she says, and then her face lights up. "Perhaps you could use a job? My husband, Mr. Gulack, owns this store. He could use some help, and I need someone to help around the house and yard. If you'd like the job, we'll pay you $3 a week plus room and board."

The money would help your family. But Papa could use your help on the farm now more than ever. In what way is your help needed most?

→ To take the job in town, turn to page 65.

→ To continue helping Papa on the farm, turn to page 70.

"Papa," you say, "We've got a good start here. We can plant even more wheat this year. The field is already plowed."

Mama says, "Haven't we traveled enough? Let's stay here and grow roots."

Papa nods. "It is settled then. We will stay."

Papa quits his job in town to devote his time to the farm. Together, you plant a large wheat crop. But the summer is hot and dry. Little rain falls, leaving your fields bone-dry. The harvest is small, and wheat prices are low.

As a few years pass, the drought continues. Some harvests are better than others. Your family has just enough money to get by.

Farmers loaded their wheat into wagons and hauled it into town to sell.

In March 1891, you turn 21. Papa says it is time for you to marry. He speaks to the matchmaker, or Koopelsmann, in Menno. After meeting with the fathers of young men and women of marrying age, the matchmaker suggests the best match. For you, he chooses the daughter of a shopkeeper. Papa approves of the choice, and the marriage is arranged. The wedding takes place in early April.

Turn the page.

Now you and your wife must begin your new life together. Should you find land of your own to farm? You know how to run a farm. True, you've had a streak of bad luck, but the drought can't last forever. When it finally ends, the harvests and the prices should improve.

On the other hand, your new father-in-law has offered you a job in his shop. Should you move to town to start an entirely new career?

⇢ *To start your own farm, turn to page **68**.*

⇢ *To learn how to run the shop in town, turn to page **69**.*

You don't want to stay in Menno if your relatives leave. "Let's go north. The land is free," you remind Papa.

"I'm told there is still plenty of land," your uncle says. "But we must hurry."

Finally, Papa nods. "We'll give homesteading a try."

You move north in a covered wagon pulled by oxen. The trip takes two weeks. Papa finds some open land near the town of Ashley and makes his claim. Your uncle claims land a little farther west.

Turn the page.

Trees and lumber were scarce on the prairie, so settlers built their homes with sod.

The first task is to plow the fields. You help lead the oxen while Papa handles the wooden plow. Your brothers plant the wheat seeds by hand.

When the planting is finished, you build a house. You help Papa and your brothers cut blocks of sod from the prairie. You all pile them like bricks to make the walls and roof. After three days, the house is completed.

Turn to page 71.

You decide to move to town. The extra cash will help your family. You weed the vegetable garden, run errands, and help keep the store tidy. You send everything you earn home. Papa and your brothers work hard on the farm. The next spring, they are able to plant a larger field of wheat.

In May 1888, the railroad announces that it will not put in tracks to Hoskins. Instead, they will go to the town of Ashley, 3 miles to the west. Ashley will be the new county seat. To be near the railroad, the people of Hoskins move everything, including houses and businesses, to Ashley.

That winter, the Gulacks send you to school. You are the oldest of eight students. But you must sit with the younger children because you are still learning English.

Turn the page.

You learn quickly. In 1889, North Dakota becomes a state, and you finish eighth grade. "I have plans for you," Mrs. Gulack says. "There is a high school in Ellendale, 40 miles east of here. My sister will give you a place to live while you go to school. In two years, you can get a teaching certificate."

"Me? A teacher?"

You visit Papa the next day. Papa expects you to become a farmer like he is. "There's always work for farmers," he says.

"And there's always work for teachers," you answer. But deep down, you're not sure what to do.

→ To become a teacher, go to page 67.
→ To become a farmer, turn to page 68.

You work for Mrs. Gulack's sister in Ellendale. After two years of high school, you get a teaching job at a country school in McIntosh County.

At first, many of your students speak German. But over time, more and more know English before they begin school. Your school grows from a one-room schoolhouse into a two-story building.

When you first reached Dakota Territory, the prairie seemed vast and empty. Now it's dotted with successful farms and busy towns. Sons and daughters of Germans own large farms, run businesses, and serve as leaders in the growing state of North Dakota.

THE END

To follow another path, turn to page 9.
To read the conclusion, turn to page 101.

You decide to become a farmer like your father and grandfather. After finding your own claim, you plow and plant a field of wheat.

The drought continues. Some years, you have a great crop. Other years, you barely scrape by.

In 1897, Niels Hansen, a plant scientist from South Dakota State University, goes to Russia to find plants better suited for dry conditions. He brings back seeds of Cossack alfalfa. You decide to give it a try.

Your alfalfa crop is a success. You buy more land and plant more seeds. Finally, you have achieved the dream that brought you and your parents to America: a successful farm of your own.

THE END

To follow another path, turn to page 9.
To read the conclusion, turn to page 101.

At your father-in-law's store in town, you sell tools, farm equipment, and animal feed. The German-Russian farmers like to trade with you. You are always fair. If times are tough, you loan them money and equipment.

Your father-in-law dies two years after you move to town. He leaves the store to you. You never become rich, but you make enough to support your family. Your children go to school in town, and all of them graduate from high school. You are proud that your children will help build South Dakota's future.

THE END

To follow another path, turn to page 9.
To read the conclusion, turn to page 101.

Horses and other animals pulled plows to break up sod for new fields.

Papa is pleased when you tell him you want to help rebuild the farm. You spend the winter tending the animals and repairing the tools. Come spring, you plant a large wheat crop.

Through the summer, the threat of fire hangs over your farm. Rain comes in small, short bursts. It's hardly enough to keep your crop alive. But somehow, the summer ends without any fires. You and Papa sigh with relief.

That fall, Papa sells the wheat. He has enough money to buy Mama some new pots, wool cloth, and more chickens.

After five years, Papa travels to the Land Office to receive the permanent title to the land. You have faced long winters and dry summers. But you never gave up, and now your determination has paid off. You and your family are landowners in America.

THE END

To follow another path, turn to page 9.
To read the conclusion, turn to page 101.

Since 1884, the Statue of Liberty has welcomed immigrants to New York.

CHAPTER 4

A World at War

"Look!" you shout. "The Statue of Liberty!"
You'll always remember this moment on July 2,
1914, as the beginning of your life in America.

America. The word itself sends a thrill
through you. It has been years since your aunts
and uncles first left Germany to go to America.
Their letters made America sound almost
magical. They told of jobs, opportunities, and
freedom. They finally convinced your parents
to join them.

But at the last minute, Grandmother got
sick. "We can't leave her," Mother said. "Your
uncles have invited you to come by yourself.
You can live with them until we can join you."

Turn the page.

"We'll follow soon," Father added.

Father made arrangements for you to travel by ship from Bremen, Germany, to New York. "From there, it is up to you," he said.

You join dozens of other travelers waiting to purchase train tickets. You leave the ship and get in line to purchase your train ticket to Wisconsin. It is time to make your choice. Uncle Paul wants you to come to Milwaukee. But Uncle Walter wants you to join his family on their farm in Watertown. You don't know much about either place. You'll just be glad to be with family again.

You reach the front of the line. "Destination?" the ticket agent asks.

➤ To choose Milwaukee, go to page **75**.

➤ To choose Watertown, turn to page **77**.

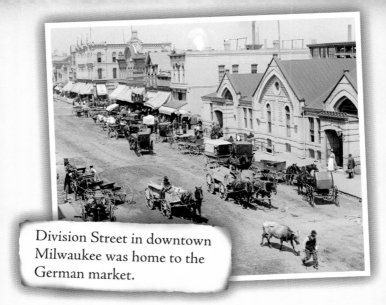

Division Street in downtown Milwaukee was home to the German market.

You go by train to Milwaukee. Uncle Paul's neighborhood reminds you of home. Signs are in German, and the streets are lined with German bookstores, grocery stores, and butcher shops.

On Sunday afternoon, Uncle takes the family to Milwaukee's most popular beer garden, Schlitz Park. "Just as they are in Germany, beer gardens in America are not just about drinking beer," your aunt says. "They are where Germans get together to share music and laughter."

Turn the page.

Lush flower gardens surround a big pavilion where dozens of families sit and visit. Aunt and Uncle join friends. You listen to Hensler's Juvenile Brass Band. This band travels all over the country playing German music at weddings and fairs.

After the concert, you wander around the park. In one area, a group from the Turnverein, or Turner's Club, gives a gymnastics demonstration. In another, a singing club performs German songs. When you tell your aunt and uncle all that you have seen, Uncle says, "Germans love clubs. We have clubs for gymnastics, singing, sharpshooting, and even for bowling."

Turn to page 79.

Uncle Walter meets you at the train depot in Watertown, Wisconsin.

You drive into the rolling countryside. Uncle stops beside a big red barn. There's also a large two-story farmhouse, a small shed for chickens, several neatly fenced fields, and woods beyond. "It's all mine," Uncle says.

In Germany, most farmers pay rent to large landowners in order to farm small sections of land. "In America, anyone, even immigrants like us, can own land," Uncle says.

Turn the page.

Milking cows was a daily chore
for dairy farmers.

There's much to do on the farm. You milk
cows and mend fences. Uncle even teaches you
to drive the wagon.

You attend church with Uncle's family. A
girl your age invites you to join the choir. "We
have singing societies in town too."

You join a singing society. They are preparing for a Saengerfest, or singing festival. The German music makes you homesick.

In late August, you receive a letter from Father. "Mother and I are well," he writes. "But we cannot come to America now." He explains that on June 28, 1914, Archduke Franz Ferdinand of Austria-Hungary was murdered. As a result, Austria-Hungary declared war on Serbia. In late July, Russia sided with Serbia. Germany then declared war on Russia. France supported Russia, so Germany declared war on them too. On August 4, the United Kingdom joined the war against the Germans. "Germany is at war. Travel will not be safe until the fighting ends," Father writes. "Pray for peace," he adds.

Turn the page.

You do as Father asks. You read about the war in Europe in the newspaper every day. The year passes slowly as you worry about Mother and Father.

In June 1915, you will graduate from high school. You must decide what to do next.

You read an article about Red Cross nurses. You could become a nurse. But your aunt wants you to attend college in New Ulm, Minnesota.

The pastor of your church offers another choice. A German immigrant in Ashland, Wisconsin, needs a German-speaking nanny.

➻ *To become a nurse, go to page 81.*

➻ *To go to college, turn to page 82.*

➻ *To become a nanny, turn to page 84.*

You enter the School of Nursing at Milwaukee County General Hospital. Many of the patients speak German. After all, Milwaukee is the most German city in America.

Meanwhile, war news covers the front pages of newspapers. On April 2, 1917, President Woodrow Wilson holds a special session of Congress. He declares war on Germany. "We must make the world safe for democracy," he says.

You are one month away from graduating from nursing school. The hospital offers you a job with good wages, but you had planned to work for the Red Cross.

➤ *To take the nursing job at the hospital, turn to page 88.*

➤ *To join the Red Cross, turn to page 90.*

You take the train to New Ulm, Minnesota. You live with your aunt and attend college at Dr. Martin Luther College. Most of the students are Germans like you.

In April 1917, President Wilson asks Congress to declare war against Germany. A few days later, the Minnesota legislature creates a Commission of Public Safety. Its goal is to stop activities that could hurt the war effort.

New Ulm, Minnesota, was founded by Germans in 1853.

In July, there's to be a rally in New Ulm's Turner Park. "I've heard that speakers will protest the war," a friend says.

When you tell your aunt, she says, "Don't go. Protesting the war is dangerous for Germans. Some members of the Commission of Public Safety consider all Germans spies."

When you tell your friend about your aunt's fears, he says, "Don't be silly. You may not be a citizen yet, but you are loyal. Besides, you are just listening to respectable local leaders give speeches in a public park. How could that be disloyal?"

➻ *To go to the meeting, turn to page 93.*

➻ *To stay away, turn to page 99.*

In Ashland, you take care of six small children. Their father, Charles, treats you kindly. There are not as many Germans in Ashland. Most people speak English.

Your uncle writes you a letter. "There is much talk of America entering the war. If America goes to war, Germans might be considered enemies. Be careful what you say and do."

Once war is declared in April 1917, people act as if everything American is good and everything German is bad.

One day, the Boy Scouts stop by to sell Liberty Bonds. "The bonds cost $50," the Scouts say. "They earn interest. After we win the war, you can cash them in. You'll make money. Meanwhile, the government will use the money to support our troops."

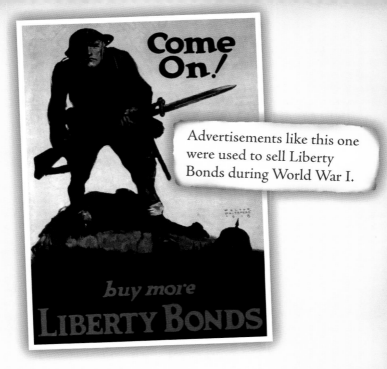

Advertisements like this one were used to sell Liberty Bonds during World War I.

Charles buys two bonds.

"Don't taxes support the soldiers?" you ask after the Scouts leave.

"There's not enough tax money to fight a big war. That's why the government sells bonds. Wars are expensive. The money we pay for bonds will support the troops."

Turn the page.

You don't have $50, but when the government comes up with a new plan, you help too. War savings certificates cost only $4.12 at the post office. "You can cash them in with interest after five years," the post office clerk says.

One day, you are visiting an old German couple on a neighboring farm when a bond salesman stops by.

"I already bought bonds," the farmer says.

"Buy more. Unless you want the Germans to win?" the salesman taunts.

"I've bought enough," the farmer says.

The salesman looks angry when he leaves. That night a mob attacks the farm and hauls the farmer to jail.

You are called as a witness at his trial. The judge asks you what the farmer said that caused such a problem. You want to defend the farmer. He's a good man. He had done what he could to help the war effort. But do you dare speak up on his behalf?

❖ To remain silent, turn to page **94**.

❖ To defend the farmer, turn to page **95**.

You send money to help the Red Cross, but take the hospital job in Milwaukee.

You remain active in your singing society. One night in November 1917, the director announces that you will no longer sing German music. "We will sing American music in English. Only English."

"Why?"

"German music is considered disloyal." The director sighs. "Beethoven is banned in Pittsburgh. New York's Metropolitan Opera won't sing German works. In California, they are cutting German folk songs out of schoolbooks."

At the hospital the next day, you treat a young man who was beaten by a mob. "They called themselves patriots," he says. "They accused me of being a spy. A spy? Me? I'm just the butcher's helper."

A sign in the butcher's window advertised hamburger. "Hamburger is German," the mob said. "Now it's called liberty steak."

In September 1918, the Spanish flu hits Milwaukee. Most of its victims are between 15 and 40 years old. Your aunt urges you to quit your job at the hospital to avoid the flu. "But I like my job," you say. "I won't get sick."

"How can you know that? Mrs. Weiss down the street needs a nurse. It's much safer."

⇒ To stay at the hospital, turn to page **97**.

⇒ To care for Mrs. Weiss, turn to page **98**.

The Red Cross sends you to France. You report to an American military hospital that houses 500 soldiers. Many have pneumonia. You rush from bed to bed giving out medicine.

One day as you walk to the hospital, you witness an air battle between French and German planes. A German plane spirals to the ground. You wonder if it might be a cousin or a former neighbor.

The war finally ends on November 11, 1918. President Wilson calls the war the "War to End All Wars." You pray he is right.

Now that the war is over, your parents will be able to come to America. It will take time, but eventually, they'll make it.

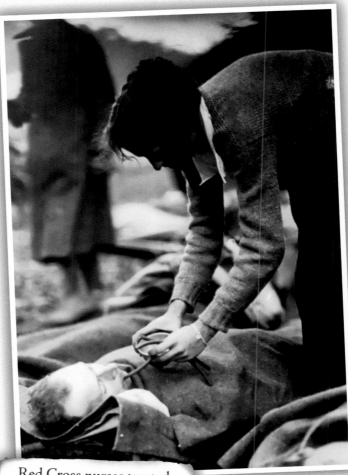

Red Cross nurses treated
wounded soldiers during
World War I.

Turn the page.

You return to Milwaukee and find work with a family doctor. You devote yourself to caring for new mothers and their babies. You like the joy and happiness of bringing new people into the world. You've seen enough sickness and death to last a lifetime.

THE END

To follow another path, turn to page 9.
To read the conclusion, turn to page 101.

You attend the rally in New Ulm's Turner Park with more than 8,000 others. Your college's president, Adolph Ackermann, suggests sending antiwar petitions to the president. He blames Britain and France for getting America involved in war.

Your friend cheers. You say nothing.

You return to your studies, but you are careful of what you say and do. President Ackermann is not so careful. He gives more speeches. A few months later, he is asked to leave the college. The Minnesota Commission of Public Safety threatens to close the college unless Ackermann leaves. Ackermann agrees to leave. Now every German in Minnesota watches what he or she says.

Turn to page **99**.

You don't dare defend the farmer. What if the mob attacks the farm where you live? The farmer is sentenced to five years in jail. You take food to his wife. "I should have defended him," you say.

"No. You could not have changed their minds. He should have been more careful. He just never bothered to take out citizenship papers. If he were a citizen, this might not have happened."

You begin to worry about your own safety. You write to your pastor, asking him to find someone to take your place. As soon as a new nanny arrives, you move back to your uncle's house until the world stops fighting.

THE END

To follow another path, turn to page 9.
To read the conclusion, turn to page 101.

Americans were encouraged to buy Liberty Bonds to help pay for the war.

You defend the farmer. "He already bought bonds. He didn't have more money to give."

The judge disagrees. "Everyone should be supporting the war efforts. He could have taken a loan. We'll feel safer if we keep this German in jail." The judge sentences the farmer to five years in prison.

Turn the page.

That night, the mob comes looking for you. "Prove you're loyal," they say. They hold out an American flag. "Kiss it," they demand.

You do what they say.

"Now buy bonds," they say.

"I don't have enough money," you protest.

One of the men is a banker. He has loan papers for you to sign. You'll be paying back the money for months to come.

You pack up and move to Milwaukee. There are so many Germans in Milwaukee that no one will even notice you. You find work in a German bookstore, sing with the church choir, and pray that someday soon the world will be at peace.

THE END

To follow another path, turn to page 9.
To read the conclusion, turn to page 101.

"I'll be fine," you say to your aunt. Wisconsin's State Health Officer, Dr. Cornelius A. Harper, issues orders to quarantine anyone who might be contagious. He closes all the schools, theaters, and churches. Everyone feels safer. Of course, people still go to work and visit friends if they feel healthy.

But you wake up one morning burning with fever and aching all over. You have the flu, and your luck has run out. You die on November 14, 1918, just three days after the war with Germany comes to an end. Of the 103,000 people in Wisconsin who catch the flu, nearly 8,500 die.

THE END

To follow another path, turn to page 9.
To read the conclusion, turn to page 101.

You agree to help the elderly German woman. One day as you shop for groceries, you notice that the Germania Bank has changed its name to the National Bank of Commerce. The paper reports other name changes. Germans are trying to become more American.

You are becoming more American too. You speak English most of the time. You will always love Germany. But all you want is for the war to end so that your parents can come to America.

As the war continues, you try to stay out of the protests and politics. You worry about your parents. Are they well? Will they ever be able to leave Germany?

What a relief it is when the war ends on November 11, 1918. People dance in the street! Your heart dances too, for soon your parents will be able to join you in America.

At first, the United States will not allow anyone to contact Germany. As soon as possible, you and others with family in Germany send food packages and other needed supplies. It will be a few years before your parents can join you, but they will come.

THE END

To follow another path, turn to page 9.
To read the conclusion, turn to page 101.

Millions of Germans came to America hoping for a better life for themselves and their children.

CHAPTER 5

German Americans

The first Germans in America were glassmakers who settled in Jamestown in 1608. Over the next 400 years, millions of German-speaking people came to America.

The largest number of German immigrants arrived between 1855 and 1890. Some came from Germany. Others came from Austria, Switzerland, and German colonies in Russia. What these immigrants had in common was the German language.

They came for reasons as individual as the Germans themselves. Some sought religious freedom, like the 13 German Quaker families who founded Germantown, Pennsylvania, in 1683. Others came for political reasons. The Germans who came to Texas in the 1840s hoped to start a German state in America. Craftsmen saw new opportunities to use their skills. Business owners wanted to open stores and factories.

Germantown was the first German settlement in America.

Most Germans, however, came in search of the American dream — a chance at a better life. Farmers dreamed of owning their own land. Through the Homestead Act of 1862, the American government offered free land for those willing to settle in the Great Plains. To lure settlers, several states set up European offices to promote themselves among German-speaking people. Letters from relatives in America described the good life to be found in the country. These "America letters" convinced many Germans to emigrate.

German immigrants often settled near other Germans. There, familiar language and culture created a sort of home away from home. While some settled in Texas or the Dakotas, most Germans came to an area called the "German Belt" that stretched from New York through Nebraska.

The German culture thrived in America until World War I. When the war began, some people feared German Americans would be loyal to Germany, not America. That fear led to prejudice against anything considered German. Instead of celebrating their German heritage, many immigrants hid it. As a result, the German way of life began to fade in America.

But the Germans left their fingerprints on American culture. Kindergartens and gymnasiums are German. German immigrants built bandstands, concert halls, playgrounds, bowling alleys, and sports clubs. They introduced the ideas of Christmas trees, Santa Claus, and the Easter bunny. Many of the foods we eat have German origins, such as hamburgers, hot dogs, granola, pretzels, and even chili powder.

The tradition of decorating a Christmas tree started with German immigrants.

Today, nearly 43 million Americans can trace their roots back to German-speaking countries. Wherever they settled, Germans brought not only their language, but also their way of life. And their ideas continue to influence us.

TIME LINE

1608 — The first Germans arrive at Jamestown, Virginia.

1683 — Thirteen German families establish Germantown, Pennsylvania.

1732 — The first German-language newspaper is published in Philadelphia.

1844 — The Adelsverein brings its first group of German settlers to Texas.

1848 — A revolution in Germany forces 4,000 to 10,000 Germans to move to the United States. This group included educated people and artists who helped establish singing societies and gymnastics clubs in the United States.

1862 — Congress passes the Homestead Act, which offers free land to settlers in the undeveloped West, particularly in Kansas, Nebraska, and Dakota Territory.

1870s — Russian Germans begin to arrive in the Midwest.

1882 — More than 250,000 Germans enter the United States.

1888 — About 800 German-language newspapers and magazines are published in the United States.

1910 — Germans farm about 100 million acres of land in the United States.

1914 — World War I begins in Europe. Russia, France, and Britain battle Germany and Austria-Hungary.

1917 — The United States enters World War I.

1918 — World War I ends.

1939 — Germany invades Poland, sparking World War II.

1940 — At least 114,000 Germans move to America to avoid German leader Adolf Hitler and the war.

1941 — The United States enters World War II against Germany, Italy, and Japan.

1945 — World War II ends.

Today — Nearly 43 million Americans claim German heritage.

OTHER PATHS TO EXPLORE

In this book, you've seen how the experiences of German immigrants were different from three points of view.

Perspectives on history are as varied as the people who lived it. You can explore other paths on your own to learn more about what happened. Seeing history from many points of view is an important part of understanding it.

Here are some ideas for other German immigration points of view to explore:

- ✦ In 1683, 13 German families arrived in America. They started a German community that came to be known as Germantown. What was life like for these families?

- ✦ During World War II, many Germans came to America to escape Adolf Hitler's brutal Nazi government. How did Americans treat them?

- ✦ Germans who immigrated to America left behind family members and other loved ones in Germany. What would it have been like to stay behind?

READ MORE

Russell, Henry. *Germany.* Washington, D.C.: National Geographic, 2007.

Trumbauer, Lisa. *German Immigrants.* New York: Facts on File, 2005.

Uschan, Michael V. *German Americans.* Milwaukee: World Almanac Library, 2007.

Yancey, Diane. *The German Americans.* San Diego: Lucent Books, 2005.

INTERNET SITES

FactHound offers a safe, fun way to find Internet sites related to this book. All of the sites on FactHound have been researched by our staff.

Here's how:

1. Visit *www.facthound.com*
2. Choose your grade level.
3. Type in this book ID **1429613564** for age-appropriate sites. You may also browse subjects by clicking on letters, or by clicking on pictures and words.
4. Click on the **Fetch It** button.

FactHound will fetch the best sites for you!

GLOSSARY

backfire (BAK-fire) — a fire started to stop a fast-moving prairie fire

immigrant (IM-uh-gruhnt) — someone who comes from abroad to live permanently in a new country

lathe (LAYTH) — a machine that holds a piece of wood or metal while turning it against a cutting tool that shapes it

pavilion (puh-VIL-yuhn) — an open building that is used for shelter or recreation or for a show or an exhibit, as in a park or at a fair

quarantine (KWOR-uhn-teen) — to keep a person, animal, or plant away from others to stop a disease from spreading

scurvy (SKUR-vee) — a deadly disease caused by lack of vitamin C; scurvy produces swollen limbs, bleeding gums, and weakness.

steppe (STEP) — vast, treeless plains found in southeastern Europe and Asia

yellow fever (YEL-oh FEE-vur) — an illness that can cause high fever, chills, nausea, and kidney and liver failure; liver failure causes the skin to become yellow, giving the disease its name.

BIBLIOGRAPHY

Adams, Willi Paul. *The German-Americans: An Ethnic Experience.* Indianapolis: Max Kade German-American Center, Indiana University-Purdue University at Indianapolis, 1993.

Biggers, Don Hampton. *German Pioneers in Texas: A Brief History of Their Hardships.* Fredericksburg, Texas: Press of the Fredericksburg Publishing Company, 1925.

Hoobler, Dorothy, and Thomas Hoobler. *The German American Family Album.* American Family Albums. New York: Oxford University Press, 1995.

Landis, Jacquelyn, ed. *The Germans.* Coming to America. San Diego: Greenhaven Press, 2006.

Luebke, Frederick C. *Bonds of Loyalty: German-Americans and World War I.* Minorities in American History. DeKalb, Ill.: Northern Illinois University Press, 1974.

Zeitlin, Richard H. *Germans in Wisconsin.* Madison, Wis.: State Historical Society of Wisconsin, 2000.

INDEX

Adelsverein, 11, 12, 14–15, 19, 21, 22, 26, 27, 28, 30, 106
Ahrens, Johann, 14, 15, 17, 34–35
America letters, 42, 73, 103
American Indians
    Comanche, 12–13, 14, 20, 23, 24–25, 27, 33, 38

beer gardens, 75
blizzards, 48, 54, 55, 56–57
Bremen, Germany, 7, 43, 74

Carlshafen, Texas, 10, 11, 14, 15, 16, 27
Civil War, 31, 32, 37
clubs, 76, 104, 106

droughts, 50, 60, 62, 68, 71

fires, 50–51, 52, 53, 58, 71
flu, 89, 97
Fredericksburg, Texas, 19, 20, 23, 24, 25, 30, 32, 33, 37, 38

Galveston, Texas, 11, 14, 17, 27, 34
Germantown, Pennsylvania, 102, 106

Hansen, Niels, 68
Homestead Act, 44, 103, 106

Kriewitz, Emil, 26, 27, 33

Liberty Bonds, 84–85, 86, 95, 96

McIntosh County, Dakota Territory, 44, 49, 58, 67
Menno, Dakota Territory, 44–45, 57, 61, 63
Meusebach, John, 17–18, 18, 19, 20, 23, 24–25, 27, 33, 38
Milwaukee, Wisconsin, 74–76, 81, 88, 89, 92, 96

New Braunfels, Texas, 15, 16, 19, 22, 28
New Ulm, Minnesota, 80, 82–83, 93

Red Cross, 80, 81, 88, 90–91
Russia, 40, 41, 42–43, 47, 49, 79, 101, 107

San Antonio, Texas, 33, 39
Sealsfield, Charles, 12
Solms-Braunfels, Prince Carl of, 15, 16

Teneger, Fritz, 36

Vereins-Kirche, 23

war savings certificates, 86
World War I, 79, 80, 81, 82–83, 84–86, 90, 91, 93, 95, 97, 98, 99, 104, 107